The Classical Singer's Christmas Album

Contents

On the recording:
* Kathleen Sonnentag, mezzo-soprano
*** duet, with Pasquale Laurino, violin
Richard Walters, pianist for the two carols
** Andrew Schroeder, baritone
Bill Casey, pianist

On the cover: El Greco, *The Adoration of the Shepherds*, oil on canvas, 42 1/2 x 34 1/4 in., The Metropolitan Museum of Art

Thank you to Maria Di Palma for her suggestions for this collection.

To access companion recorded performances and piano accompaniments online, visit:
www.halleonard.com/mylibrary

Enter Code
1183-2855-2470-0234

ISBN 978-0-7935-7006-5

HAL•LEONARD®
CORPORATION
7777 W. BLUEMOUND RD. P.O. BOX 13819 MILWAUKEE, WI 53213

Visit Hal Leonard Online at
www.halleonard.com

ON THE RECORDING

KATHLEEN SONNENTAG, mezzo-soprano, has performed a large and varied repertoire of concert works and oratorio with such conductors as Lukas Foss, Zdenek Macal, Stanislaw Skrowaczewski, Margaret Hawkins, Neal Gittleman and Robert Page. She was one of a handful of singers selected by Marilyn Horne to participate in a series of high-profile master classes at Carnegie Hall in New York. Ms. Sonnentag's many awards include the Eleanor Steber Music Foundation Award for Excellence in the Concert Field. Her many opera roles include the title role in *La Cenerentola* and Cherubino. Ms. Sonnentag may be heard on several Hal Leonard releases, including *Wedding Classics, Popular Ballads for Classical Singers, Classical Carols, Sacred Classics,* and *Songs of Joseph Marx.*

ANDREW SCHROEDER, baritone, is a singer with a significant repertoire of opera roles, and has performed with many companies. His operatic training included residencies at the Lyric Center for American Artists at Lyric Opera of Chicago, and the Metropolitan Opera's Young Artist Development Program. He received a Sullivan award in 1991. Mr. Schroeder also may be heard on the Hal Leonard releases *Sacred Classics, Wedding Classics* and *Popular Ballads for Classical Singers.*

BILL CASEY, pianist, holds degrees in piano performance from Louisiana State University and the University of Missouri/Kansas City Conservatory of Music. He is director of a music school in Kansas City, and has a working studio as a vocal coach and accompanist. Mr. Casey is also a performing tenor. He was an assistant editor on the *G. Schirmer Opera Anthology.* He also may be heard on a series of brass solos with members of The Canadian Brass, and on *Sacred Classics,* all released by Hal Leonard.

RICHARD WALTERS, pianist and arranger, is a composer who specializes in writing music for the voice. His principal composition studies were with Dominick Argento. He is Vice President of Classical and Vocal Publications at Hal Leonard. Mr. Walters is editor of many publications, including *The Singer's Musical Theatre Anthology, The Oratorio Anthology, English Songs: Renaissance to Baroque, The Singer's Movie Anthology,* and editions of the songs of Fauré, Brahms and Strauss. His concert arrangements for solo voice may be found in the collections *Classical Carols, Hymn Classics,* and *Popular Ballads for Classical Singers.*

The
Classical Singer's
Christmas Album

O HOLY NIGHT

(Cantique de Noël)

Adolphe Adam

pin - - - ing, Till he ap-pear'd, and the soul felt its
nel - - - le Et de son père ar - rê - ter le cour-

worth.
roux.

A thrill of hope the
Le mon - de en - tier tres -

cresc.

wear - y world re-joic - es, For yon - der breaks a
sail - le d'es - pé - ran - ce A cet - te nuit qui

cresc.

new and glo - rious morn. _____ Fall _____ on your
lui donne un sau - veur. _____ Peu - - ple, à ge -

f

f

knees! _____ Oh hear _____ the an - gel
noux! _____ at - tends _____ ta dé - li -

voi - ces! O night _____ di -
vran - ce. No - ël! _____ No -

vine! _____ O night _____ when Christ was
ël! _____ voi - ci _____ le Ré - demp -

cresc.

born, _____ O night _____ di -
teur, _____ No - ël! _____ No -

cresc.

vine! _____ O night, O _____ night di -
ël! _____ voi - ci le _____ Ré - demp -

dim.

vine.
teur.

mf

Led by the
De no - tre

light _____ of Faith se - rene - ly beam - ing, With glow - ing
foi _____ que la lu - mière ar - den - te nous gui - de

hearts   by   his cra - dle   we stand;
tous   au   ber- ceau   de   l'en - fant,

So,   led   by light   of   a   star   sweet - ly
comme   au - tre- fois   une   é - toi - le   bril -

gleam - ing,   Here came   the   wise   men from_____   the   O - rient
lan - te   y con - dui - sit   les   chefs_____   de   l'o - ri -

land.   The   King   of   Kings   lay
ent.   Le   Roi   des   Rois   naît

cresc.

thus in low - ly man - ger, In all our trials is
dans une hum - ble crè - che; puis - sants du jour, is fiers

f

born to be our friend; _____ He _____ knows our
de vo - tre gran - deur, _____ à _____ vo - tre or -

need, _____ to our weak - ness no
gueil _____ c'est de là _____ qu'un Dieu

stran - ger; Be - hold _____ your
prê - che; cour - bez _____ vos

broth - er, And in His name____ all op - pres - sion shall
cla - ve, L'a - mour u - nit____ ceux qu'en-chaî - nait le

cease.
fer.

Sweet hymns of joy in
Qui lui di - ra no -

grate - ful cho - rus raise we, Let all with - in us
tre re - con - nais-san - ce? C'est pour nous tous qu'il

praise His Ho - ly name. ____
naît, qu'il souf - fre et meurt. ____

Fall ____ on your
Peu - - ple, de -

THE VIRGIN'S SLUMBER SONG
(Mariä Wiegenlied)

Martin Boelitz

Max Reger

Zu ih - ren Fü - ssen singt ein bun - tes Vö - ge - lein:
And soft and sweet - ly sings a bird __ up - on the bough:

Schlaf', Kind - lein, sü - - - - sse,
Ah, ba - by, dear __ one,

schlaf' __ nun ein!
slum - - - ber now!

Hold __ ist dein Lä - cheln, hol - der dei - nes
Hap - py is Thy laugh - ter, ho - ly is __ Thy

ERMUNTRE DICH, MEIN SCHWACHER GEIST

(My Weary Spirit Braces Now)

Johann Crüger (1648)

Johann Sebastian Bach

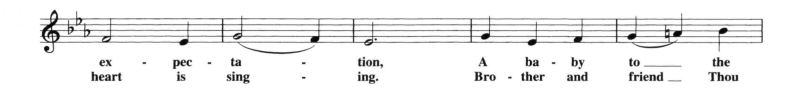

My wea - ry spi - rit brac - es now, cheer - ing with
Lord Je - sus Christ, __ all thanks to Thee my grate - ful

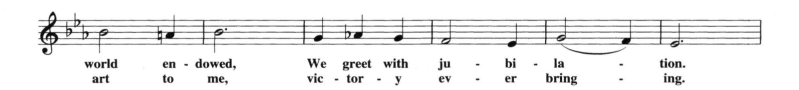

ex - pec - ta - tion, A ba - by to __ the
heart is sing - ing. Bro - ther and friend __ Thou

world en - dowed, We greet with ju - bi - la - tion.
art to me, vic - tor - y ev - er bring - ing.

The time draws nigh, __ He comes __ this night, In a mere
Help me to trust __ Thy ho - ly grace, Thy lov - ing

man __ the one __ true light. The world re - ceives sal -
mer - cy and spi - rit em - brace. In heav - en high a -

va - tion, Each soul in glad ad - o - ra - tion.
bove me, May I some day ev - er love Thee.

ERMUNTRE DICH, MEIN SCHWACHER GEIST
(My Weary Spirit Braces Now)

Johann Crüger (1648)

Johann Sebastian Bach

Dies ist die Nacht, ___ dar - in ___ es kam
Hilf, dass ich dei - ne Gü - tig - keit

und mensch - lich We - sen an ___ sich nahm, da -
stets preis' in die - ser Gna - den - zeit und

durch die Welt mit Treu - en
mög' her - nach dort o - ben

als sei - ne Braut zu ___ frei - en.
in E - wig - keit dich ___ lo - ben.

O JESULEIN SÜSS

(O Jesus So Sweet)

Hall 1650

Johann Sebastian Bach

O Je - su - lein süss,   o
O Je - su - lein süss,   o
O Je - su - lein süss,   o

Je - su - lein mild, dein's Va - ters
Je - su - lein mild, dein's Va - ters
Je - su - lein mild, mit Freud' hast

Will'n   hast   du _____ er - füllt,   bist
Zorn   hast   du _____ ge - stillt,   du
du   die   Welt _____ er - füllt,   du

O JESULEIN SÜSS

(O Jesus So Sweet)

Hall 1650

Johann Sebastian Bach

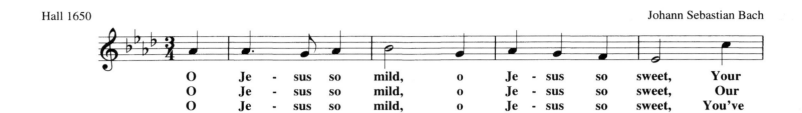

O   Je - sus so   mild,   o   Je - sus so   sweet,   Your
O   Je - sus so   mild,   o   Je - sus so   sweet,   Our
O   Je - sus so   mild,   o   Je - sus so   sweet,   You've

Fa - ther's will   did   you ___ com - plete.   From heav - en's rich - es
world - ly   sins   did   you ___ de - feat.   Be - cause you   lived the
giv - en   us   a   joy ___ re - plete.   From heav'n a - bove you

to   de - scend   and   live   as   mor - tal   man's   true friend,   O
Fa - ther's will our souls' sal - va - tion is   ful - filled,   O
came to   earth to   give us   life   in   our   re - birth,   O

Je - sus so   mild,   o   Je - sus so   sweet.
Je - sus so   mild,   o   Je - sus so   sweet.
Je - sus so   mild,   o   Je - sus so   sweet.

I STAND HERE AT THE CRADLESIDE

(Ich steh an deiner Krippe hier)

Paul Gerhard

Sigfrid Karg-Elert

VIOLIN

The violin part may be carefully cut from the book.

I STAND HERE AT THE CRADLESIDE

(Ich steh an deiner Krippe hier)

Paul Gerhard

Sigfrid Karg-Elert

Calmly and simply (not too slow)

Voice I

mp

Ich steh an dei — ner ___ Krip — pe heir, o
I stand here at ___ the ___ cra — dle's side With

Je — su, ___ du mein Le — ben, ich ___ kom — me, ___ bring und
those who ___ would a — dore you, I ___ come, ___ dear ___ Lord, a —

schen — ke ___ dir, was du mir ___ hast ge — ge — ben.
while ___ to ___ bide, To lay my ___ gifts be — fore ___ You.

Violin (ad lib.)
espressivo

Voice II

Ich lag in tief - ster__ To - des - nacht, du wur - dest__ mei - ne
When I lay bound__ in __ deep - est night, The gloom of __ death de -

Son - ne, die__ Son - ne, __ die mir zu - ge - bracht Licht,
scend - ing, 'Twas__ You, __ dear__ Lord, who gave__ me __ light, Brought

Le - ben, __ Freud und Won - ne.
life and__ joy un - end - ing.

non marcato

with growing expression

34

Schlafendes Jesuskind

(Gem älde von Francesco Albani)

Sohn der Jungfrau, Himmelskind!
am Boden auf dem Holz
    der Schmerzen eingeschlfaden,
Das der fromme Meister
    sinnvoll spielend,
Deinen leichten Träumen unterlegte;
Blume du, noch,
    in der Knospe dämmernd
Eingehüllt die Herrlichkeit des Vaters!
O wer sehen könnte, welche Bilder
Hinter dieser Stirne, diesen schwarzen
Wimpern sich in sanftem Wechsel malen!

The Sleeping Baby Jesus

(after a painting by Francesco Albani)

Son of the Virgin, Child of Heaven!
Asleep on the ground
    upon the wood of torture,
which the good Master,
    with effortless significance,
laid under your peaceful dreams.
You are the flower,
    even in the bud
showing the Father's glory.
O who could see what visions
behind this brow, these dark
lashes, are seen in this gentle succession.

SCHLAFENDES JESUSKIND
(The Sleeping Baby Jesus)

Eduard Friedrich Mörike

Hugo Wolf

Sehr getragen und weihevoll

ppp

softly

Sohn der Jung-frau, Him-mels-kind!

am Bo-den auf dem Holz__ der Schmer-zen ein-ge-schla-fen,

das der from-me Mei-ster sinn-voll spie-lend dei-nen

leich - ten Träu-men un - ter - leg - te;

sehr ausdrucksvoll
(with great expression)

Blu - me du, noch in der Knos - pe däm - mernd ein -

- ge - hüllt die Herr - lich - keit des Va - ters!

sehr innig
(very fervently)

O wer se - hen könn - te, wel - che Bil - der hin - ter

JESUS OF NAZARETH

A. Porte

Charles Gounod

Né dans u - ne crê - che, di - vin Ré - demp -
Tho' poor be the cham - ber, come here, come and a -

teur, _____ i - ci - bas __ je prê - che,
dore; _____ Lo! the Lord __ of Heav - en

i - ci - bas __ je prê - che les __ ver - tus du cœur,
hath to mor - tals giv - en life __ for ev - er more,

les ver-tus du cœur, les ver-tus du cœur.
life for-ev-er-more, life for ev-er-more.
p
mf
N'é-touf-fez
Shep-herds who
p
p
plus la voix des saints o-ra-cles; pes-ti-fé-
fold-ed your flocks be-side you, Tell what was
rés, lé-preux du la-za-reth, Es-poir en
told by an-gel voic-es near: To you this
f

les __ ver -tus du cœur. __
life __ for - ev - er - more. __

Plein de pi - tié pour la fem me a - dul -
Kings de from a far land, draw near and __ be -

tè - re qui s'a - ge - nouil - le et pleu - re en mon che -
hold Him, Led by the beam whose warn - ing bade ye

min, __ Je dis à ceux qui lui
come; __ Your crowns cast down, __ with

pp

jet - tent la pier - re, sur vo - tre
robe roy - al en - fold Him; Your King de -

cœur a - vez - vous mis la main?
scends to earth from bright - er home.

poco rit.

pp a tempo

Né dans u - ne crê - che, di - vin Ré - demp - teur,
Tho' poor be the cham - ber, come here, come and a - dore;

i - ci bas je prê - che, i - ci bas je prê - che
Lo! the Lord of Heav - en hath to mor - tals giv - en

45

les ___ ver - tus du cœur. _____
life ___ for - ev - er - more. _____

A - veu - gles nés, _____ mu -
Wind, to the ce - dars pro -

ets, pa - ra - ly - ti - ques, pau - vres per -
claim the joy - ful sto - ry; Wave of the

dus, boi - teux, sourds ap - pro - chez. _____ Du
sea, _____ boi - teux, the ti - dings bear a - far. _____ The

THE BIRTHDAY OF A KING

W. H. Neidlinger

ho - ly light, O'er the place where Je - sus lay: Al - le -

lu - ia!_____ O how the an - gels sang, Al - le - lu - ia! how it

rang; And the sky was bright with a

ho - ly light, 'Twas the birth-day of a King.

way: Al - le - lu - ia! ____ O how the an - gels sang, Al - le -

lu - ia! how it rang; And the

sky was bright with a ho - ly light, 'Twas the

birth - day of a King.

IN THE BLEAK MIDWINTER

Christina Rossetti

Gustav Holst
Arranged by Richard Walters

Snow had fall - en snow on snow, Snow____ on____

snow, In the bleak mid - win - - ter

Long _____ a - go.

An - gels and arch - an - gels May have gath - ered

there, Che - ru - bim and ser - a - phim

Throng - ed the air; But his moth - er

on - ly, In her maid - en bliss,

Wor - shipped the be - lov - ed With_____ a

p

decresc.

If I were a wise man,

I would do my part; Yet what I can I

give him: _____ Give _____ my

heart. _____

SILENT NIGHT

Joseph Mohr
English translation by John F. Young

Franz Gruber
Arranged by Richard Walters

keep pedal down

58

hei - li - ge Paar. Hol - der Kna - be im lo - cki -gen Haar, Schlaf in

himm - lisch-er Ruh, _____ Schlaf _ in himm - lisch-er Ruh. _____

p

Si - lent night, Ho - ly night! All is

calm, All is bright Round yon vir - gin Moth - er and

Selections from The Vocal Library

The Oratorio Anthology
00747058 Soprano
00747059 Alto/Mezzo-Soprano
00747060 Tenor
00747061 Baritone/Bass

Songs of Claude Debussy
critical edition
00660164 High Voice
00660283 Medium Voice

Gabriel Fauré: 50 Songs
00747071 High Voice
00747070 Medium/Low Voice

Songs of Joseph Marx
with companion CD
00747027 High Voice
00747026 Medium Voice

Mozart Arias
with companion
accompaniment CD
00740042 Soprano
00740043 Mezzo-Soprano
00740044 Tenor
00740045 Baritone/Bass

Johannes Brahms: 75 Songs
00740013 High Voice
00740015 Low Voice

Early Puccini for Soprano
00747028
five arias from *Le Villi* and *Edgar*

Puccini: Two Arias from
La Rondine
00747029

Richard Strauss: 40 Songs
00747062 High Voice
00747063 Medium/Low Voice

Classical Carols
concert arrangements
with companion CD
00747024 High Voice
00747025 Low Voice

The Classical Singer's
Christmas Album
with companion CD
00740062 High Voice
00740063 Low Voice

Favorite French Art Songs
with companion CD
00740046 High Voice
00740047 Low Voice

Favorite German Art Songs
with companion CD
00740048 High Voice
00740049 Low Voice

Hymn Classics
concert arrangements
with companion CD
00740033 High Voice
00740032 Low Voice

Italian Tenor Arias
with companion CD
00740050

Sacred Classics
with companion CD
00740051 High Voice
00740052 Low Voice

English Songs:
Renaissance To Baroque
00740018 High Voice
00740019 Low Voice

Wedding Classics
with companion CD
00740053 High Voice
00740054 Low Voice

12 Wedding Songs
for voice and guitar
00740007 Medium Voice

Popular Ballads
for Classical Singers
with companion recording
00660204 High Voice
00660205 Low Voice

FOR MORE INFORMATION, SEE YOUR LOCAL MUSIC DEALER,
OR WRITE TO:

HAL•LEONARD®
CORPORATION
7777 W. BLUEMOUND RD. P.O. BOX 13819 MILWAUKEE, WI 53213